New York yacht-racing association

Constitution and By-Laws, Sailing Regulations, Rules and Time Allowances of the New York Yacht Racing Association

Vol. 2

New York yacht-racing association

Constitution and By-Laws, Sailing Regulations, Rules and Time Allowances of the New York Yacht Racing Association
Vol. 2

ISBN/EAN: 9783337407278

Printed in Europe, USA, Canada, Australia, Japan

Cover: Foto ©Suzi / pixelio.de

More available books at **www.hansebooks.com**

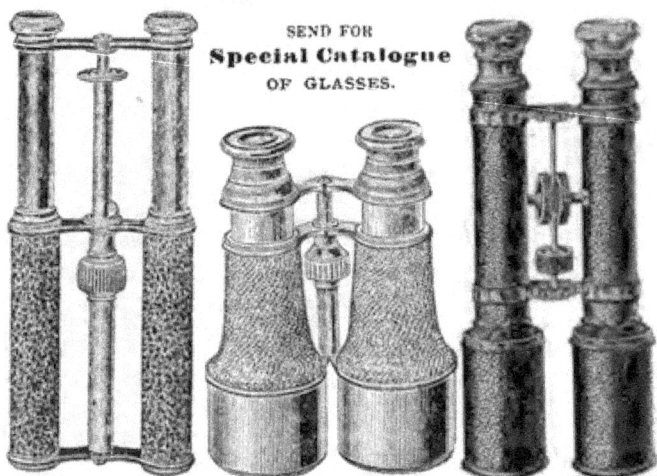

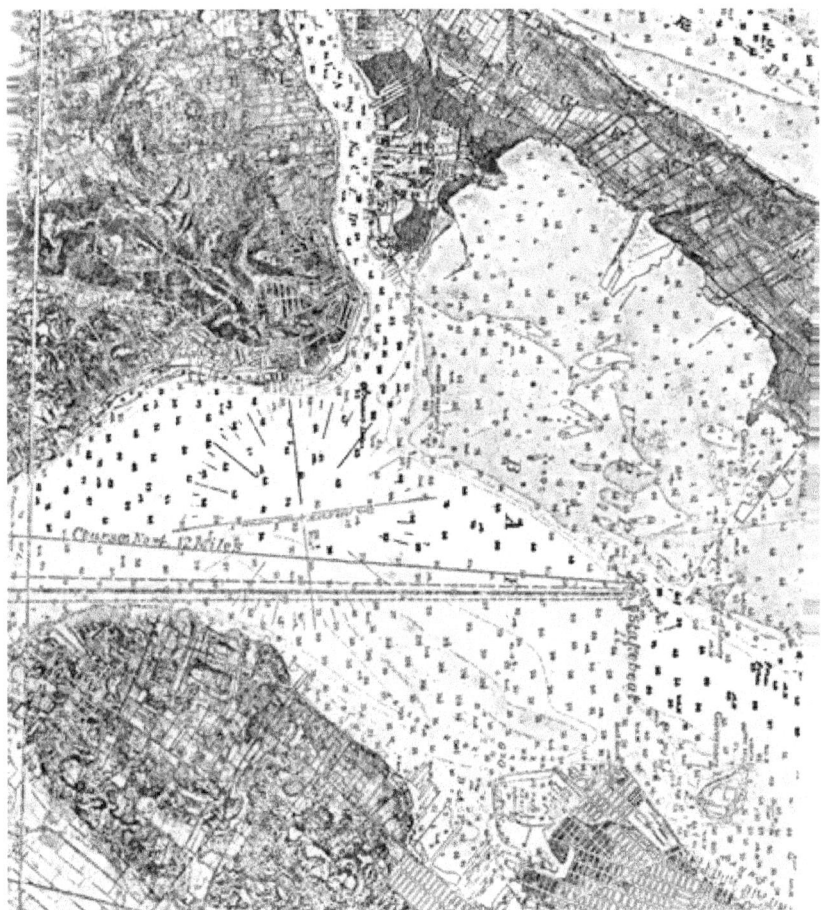

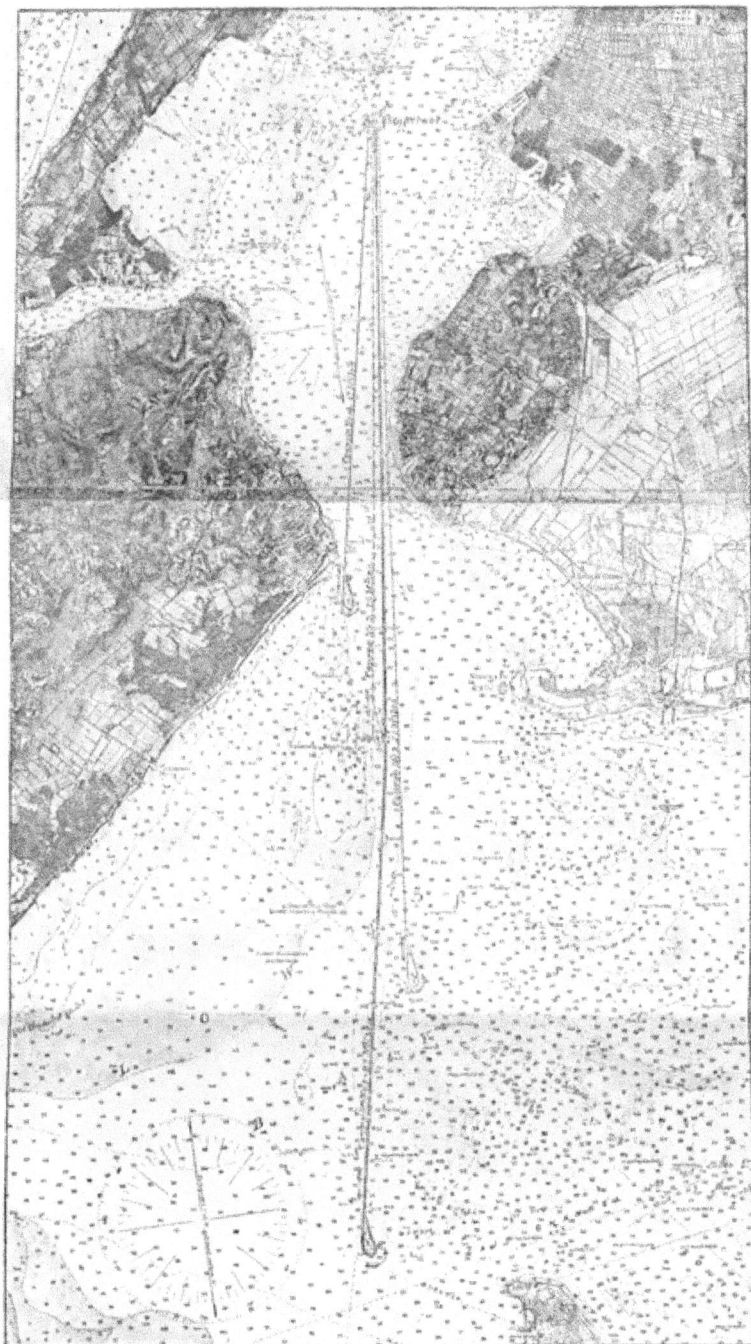

NEW YORK YACHT RACING ASSOCIATION.—COURSES.

Course 1, Classes A, B, C, D, E
    and F, ...27 miles.

Course 2, Classes G, H, 1, 2, 4,
    6 and 7, ...21 miles.

Course 3, Classes 3, 5, 8
    and 9, ...15 miles.

Course 4, Class 10........
    ....12 miles.

CONSTITUTION and BY-LAWS,

SAILING REGULATIONS, RULES AND

TIME ALLOWANCES

—OF THE—

NEW YORK

Yacht Racing Association.

ORGANIZED MARCH 8, 1889.

INCORPORATED AUGUST 15, 1889.

With List of Yacht Clubs Enrolled in Same,

—AND A—

*DIRECTORY OF PROMINENT DEALERS
IN VARIOUS KINDS OF MATERIAL FOR
USE IN CONSTRUCTING AND RE-
PAIRING SAILING AND STEAM
YACHTS, LAUNCHES, ETC.*

·1892.

USE WOOLSEY'S

COPPER **BEST** PAINT

WHY?

"Because it is **the only Copper Paint**
that will keep the bottoms of wooden vessels clean
for one year, and we guarantee this or will repaint

LIST OF YACHT CLUBS

BELONGING TO THE

• NEW YORK · YACHT · RACING · ASSOCIATION. •

BAYSWATER YACHT CLUB......Bayswater, N. Y.
BROOKLYN YACHT CLUB.......Brooklyn, N. Y.
CANARSIE YACHT CLUB.........Canarsie, N. Y.
COLUMBIA YACHT CLUB.............New York.
HARLEM YACHT CLUB.............. New York.
HUDSON RIVER YACHT CLUB........New York.
INDIAN HARBOR YACHT CLUB, Greenwich, Conn.
JERSEY CITY YACHT CLUB....Jersey City, N. J.
KILL VON KULL YACHT CLUB,
                    Port Richmond, S. I., N. Y.
NEWARK YACHT CLUB............Newark, N. J.
NEWARK BAY YACHT CLUB......Bayonne, N. J.
NEW JERSEY YACHT CLUB......Hoboken, N. J.
NORTH SHREWSBURY YACHT CLUB,
                    Red Bank, N. J.
OCEANIC YACHT CLUB. ......Jersey City, N. J.
PAVONIA YACHT CLUB. ....Jersey City, N. J.
SING SING YACHT CLUB........Sing Sing, N. Y.
STATEN ISLAND ATHLETIC CLUB,
    (Yachting Department,) West New Brighton, S. I.
TAPPAN ZEE YACHT CLUB...Grand View, N. Y.
WILLIAMSBURGH YACHT CLUB....Astoria, L. I.
YONKERS CORINTHIAN YACHT CLUB,
                    Yonkers, N. Y.

OFFICERS OF THE ASSOCIATION.
1892.

————◆————

PRESIDENT,
ALANSON J. PRIME,
Commodore, Yonkers Corinthian Yacht Club.

VICE-PRESIDENT,
GEORGE E. GARTLAND,
Of the New Jersey Yacht Club.

SECRETARY,
GEORGE PARKHILL,
Of the Columbia Yacht Club.

TREASURER,
ROBERT K. McMURRAY,
Of the Staten Island Athletic Club.

EXECUTIVE COMMITTEE,
C. H. BENSON,
Commodore, Jersey City Yacht Club.

DANIEL O'REILLY,
President Brooklyn Yacht Club.

WM. A. SMITH,
Vice Commodore, Pavonia Yacht Club.

A. N. BACON,
Of the Harlem Yacht Club.

ISRAEL F. FISCHER,
Commodore, Canarsie Yacht Club.

CONSTITUTION.

ARTICLE I.

NAME.

The name of this Association shall be the "NEW YORK YACHT RACING ASSOCIATION."

ARTICLE II.

OBJECTS.

The objects of this Association shall be: To encourage yacht building and yacht racing; to establish and enforce uniform rules for the government of all races in which two or more clubs, members of the Association, shall compete.

ARTICLE III.

MEMBERSHIP.

Any yacht club located in the States of New York, New Jersey and Connec-

PATENT
PUMP WATER CLOSET,
For Yachts, Launches, Pilot Boats, Etc.

Manufacturers of Yacht and Ship Water Closets, Bilge, Tank, Deck, Sink and Basin Pumps, Galvanized Iron and Copper Tanks, Hand and Deep Sea Leads, Brass and Copper Ventilators.

FOR ABOVE OR BELOW WATER LINE.

Patented and Manufactured by

ALFRED B. SANDS & SON,

Plumbers; Steam Fitters & Coppersmiths,
134 BEEKMAN STREET,
NEW YORK CITY.

Yacht Plumbing a Specialty.

ticut in good standing, having twenty-five members and ten yachts, measuring more than sixteen feet in length on the water line, shall be eligible to membership.

Application for membership must be made in writing to the Secretary of the Association, must be signed by the Commodore or the Secretary of the club applying for membership, and must contain a correct list of the members and yachts of the club.

The Executive Committee shall act upon said application, and may admit any clubs eligible under this article. The decision of the Committee shall be final.

ARTICLE IV.

REPRESENTATION.

Each club shall be represented in the Association by three delegates, but shall have but one vote.

Telephone Call, 2143 "Cortlandt."

OWAIN L. HUGHES,

YACHT BROKER,

34 NEW STREET AND 58 BROAD STREET,

NEW YORK.

Agent by Appointment for the Sale of

U. S. Coast and Geodetic Charts and Publications.

ARTICLE V.

OFFICERS.

The officers of the Association shall be as follows: President, Vice-President, Secretary, Treasurer and an Executive Committee consisting of five members, of which the President and Vice-President shall be members *ex-officio*.

The officers shall be elected by ballot at the annual meetings, and shall hold office for one year, or until their successors have been elected.

Vacancies may be filled at any regular or special meeting. A majority of the votes of the clubs present shall be necessary to elect.

ARTICLE VI.

DUTIES OF OFFICERS.

President.

The President shall preside at all meetings, and enforce all rules and regu-

JAMES HAMMOND,

SAIL MAKER

399 WEST ST.,

NEW YORK.

YACHT SAILS A SPECIALTY.

AWNINGS, TENTS, &c.,

Made to Order.

New and Old Secondhand Sails

——AND——

Old Canvas Constantly on Hand.

lations of the Association. He may call a special meeting at his pleasure, and shall do so at the written request of any three clubs of the Association.

Vice-President.

The Vice-President shall assist the President in the discharge of his duties, and in his absence shall officiate in his stead.

Secretary.

The Secretary shall keep a true record of the proceedings of all the meetings of the Association in a book provided for that purpose; shall keep a correct roll of all the clubs and delegates; shall notify every delegate of every meeting; shall collect all moneys due to the Association and pay the same over to the Treasurer, taking his receipt therefor.

Treasurer.

The Treasurer shall receive all moneys

collected by the Secretary for the Association, giving his receipt therefor, and pay all bills contracted by it and approved by a majority of the members of the Executive Committee, keeping a correct account of the same in a book provided for that purpose. He shall make a report at each annual meeting of all the receipts and expenditures, and of the amount of money remaining on hand.

Executive Committee.

The Executive Committee shall act as a Membership Committee; shall establish and enforce penalties for the infringement of the racing rules of the Association, and shall settle any dispute arising out of the construction of racing rules which shall be referred to the Association; and the Executive Committee shall, in the case of protest or dispute, appoint some qualified person to act as Measurer, whose meas-

urement shall be final and binding on all interested.

ARTICLE VII.

MEETINGS.

There shall be an annual meeting on the first Wednesday in February in each year, at which reports of the Secretary and Treasurer shall be read, and officers for the ensuing year shall be elected.

Special meetings may be called by order of the President. Notice of each meeting shall be issued by the Secretary four days before the date thereof.

Representatives from five clubs shall constitute a quorum. Voting by proxy shall not be allowed, but in case of the absence of any delegate, his place at that meeting may be filled in such a manner as his club may have provided.

MANUFACTURED BY

EMIL CALMAN & CO.,
299 Pearl Street, New York.

Read what some of the principal boat and ship builders say of our Spar Varnishes:

———o———

BRISTOL, R. I., April 9, '90.

EMIL CALMAN & CO., 299 Pearl St., New York.

Gentlemen:—We have given your Elastic Spar Varnish a thorough trial, and some very severe tests, and it has given us satisfaction on all work we have put it on.

Among the boats we have used it upon we may mention the steam yachts "Augusta," "Daisy" and "Judy," also the U. S. Torpedo Boat No. 1, "Cushing."

We are very much pleased with it, and shall continue to use it.   Respectfully,

HERRESHOFF MFG. CO.

———o———

Messrs. EMIL CALMAN & Co.

Gentlemen:—It gives me pleasure to state that your Spar Varnish was used on "Volunteer," "Mayflower," "Gundred," and other boats of my design, and has given much satisfaction.   Yours truly,

EDWARD BURGESS.

22 CONGRESS ST., BOSTON, March 1, '88.

FOR SALE BY ALL DEALERS.

ARTICLE VIII.

ASSESSMENTS.

Funds for defraying the current expenses of the Association shall be raised by an annual assessment on each club of Ten Dollars, which shall be due and payable in advance, and the financial year shall begin at the date of the Annual Meeting. No other assessments shall be levied except by a two-thirds vote of all the clubs present at a meeting called for that purpose.

ARTICLE IX.

WITHDRAWALS.

The membership of any club in the Association shall be forfeited by voluntary withdrawal, or by a two-thirds vote of all the clubs in the Association, at a meeting specially called, at which such club shall have an opportunity to be heard in its own defense.

ARTICLE X.

AMENDMENTS.

This Constitution may be amended by a two-thirds vote of all the clubs of the Association, at any meeting of the Association; provided, however, that the notice of such meeting shall have contained the proposed amendment in full.

BY - LAWS,

Sailing Rules and Regulations

BY-LAWS.

ARTICLE I.

ORDER OF BUSINESS.

The following order of business shall be observed, and shall not be departed from except by a two-thirds vote :

1. Roll call.
2. Minutes of previous Meeting.
3. Report of Secretary.
4. Report of Treasurer.
5. Report of Executive Committee.
6. Report of Select Committees.
7. Election of Officers.
8. Unfinished Business.
9. New Business.

RULES OF ORDER.

The following rules of order shall be observed at all meetings of this Association:

1. Any member wishing to speak shall rise and address the Chair. If two or more members shall claim the floor at the same time, the Chair shall decide who is entitled to it.

2. No motion can be entertained by the Chair unless seconded; and until decided no other motion shall be in order, except for the previous question, or to lay on the table, to amend, re-commit or adjourn.

3. All motions and resolutions must be produced in writing, if required by any member present.

4. When a question is put, every club present shall vote, unless personally interested or excused by the Chair. No member shall move a reconsideration of

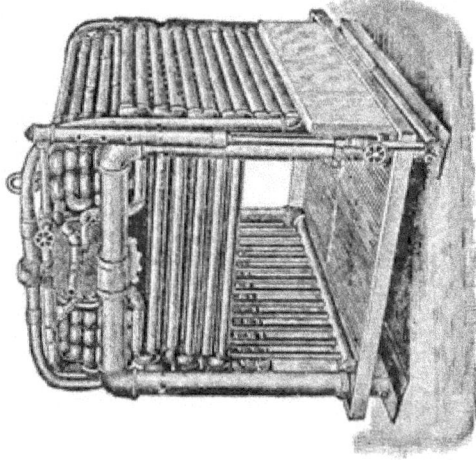

any vote unless he voted with the majority which decided the question.

5. Any member may appeal to the meeting from the decision of the Chair, and if seconded the question shall be: "Shall the decision of the Chair ·be sustained?"

6. No member shall speak more than twice on the same question without permission of the meeting.

7. When the floor is not occupied, a motion to adjourn is always in order, and it is not debatable.

8. Any two clubs may call for the yeas and nays upon any debatable motion, and the Secretary shall call the names of the members present and enroll the vote.

9. Any of the foregoing Rules of Order may be suspended at any meeting by a two-thirds vote of the clubs present, but

such suspension shall terminate with the meeting.

10. Cushing's Manual shall be authority for the construction of the foregoing rules, and to decide disputed questions of order not herein provided for.

ARTICLE II.

MEASUREMENT FOR TIME ALLOWANCE.

The measurement for allowance of time shall be the length on deck, measured from the forward part of the stem to the extreme stern over all; to this is to be added the length of the load water line, measured when in sailing trim, the two measurements to be added together and divided by two. The result thus obtained shall be the sailing length.

ARTICLE III.

ASSOCIATION BOOKS.

There shall be printed each year, under

the direction of the Secretary, books for
the use of each member of the Association,
containing the Constitution, By-Laws,
Sailing Regulations, etc., of the Association, together with a list of all the clubs
belonging to the same, and shall contain
a chart of the Association pennant and
the respective club flags ; and for this purpose the Secretary is required to obtain
from the clubs belonging to the Association, the respective cuts of their club
signals.

REMARKABLE FACT.

THIS cut is a copy of a photograph of a board having one end painted with New Jersey Copper Paint, manufactured by Harry Louderbough, New Jersey Paint Works, Jersey City, N. J., and placed in the water at Port Royal, S. C. for five months. Upon the unpainted end you can note the ravages of the salt water worm, so destructive to wood, and also the large number of barnacles that have fastened upon it. Observe the painted end, where New Jersey Copper Paint was applied—its splendid condition.

—OUR—

Marine Paint Specialties:

NEW JERSEY.

- Copper Paint.
- Red Copper Paint,
  - For Yachts.
- Elastic Seam Paint.
- Yacht Black.
- Yacht White,
- Mast Paint.
- Smoke Stack Paint.
- Deck and Floor Paint.

The American Institute Fair of New York has awarded us the highest attainable Medal for our Marine Paint Specialties.

NEW JERSEY
COPPER PAINT.

RACING RULES.

MANAGEMENT OF RACES.

All races, and all yachts sailing therein, shall be under the direction of the Regatta Committee of the club under whose auspices the races are being sailed, or of officers appointed to take charge for the day. All matters shall be subject to their approval and control, and all doubts, questions and disputes which may arise, shall be subject to their decision. Their decision shall be based upon these rules so far as they will apply, but as no rules can be devised capable of meeting every incident and accident of sailing, the Regatta Committee should keep in view the ordinary customs of the sea, and discourage all attempts to win a race by other means than fair sailing and

superior speed and skill. The decisions of the Regatta Committee or officers in charge of the race shall be final, unless they think fit, on the application of the parties interested, or otherwise, to refer the questions at issue for the decision of the Executive Committee of the New York Yacht Racing Association. No member of the Regatta Committee or of the Executive Committee, or of the Judges, shall take part in the decision upon any disputed question in which he is directly interested. The Regatta Committee, or any officers appointed to take charge for the day, shall award the prizes. If any yacht be disqualified, the next in order shall be awarded the prize.

RULE I.

CLASSIFICATION.

In all regattas given by clubs belonging to this Association, the classification

THE ELYSIAN BOAT WORKS,
FOURTEENTH ST., HOBOKEN, N. J.

A. HANSEN,
Yacht Designer and Builder.

——ALL CLASSES OF——

YACHTS, STEAM LAUNCHES,
SINGLE HAND CRUISERS. KEEL
OR CENTER BOARD,
LIFE BOATS, YAWLS, AND
WHITEHALL BOATS.

MARINE RAILWAYS.

Yachts hauled out and taken care of during Winter.

ALL KINDS OF REPAIRING ATTENDED TO PROMPTLY.

Builder of Sloop CARRIE B., winner in respective class
of the New York Yacht Racing Association, 1891.

shall be made as such club may deem
best; but in all regattas given by the
Association, the classification shall be observed as follows :

CLASS A—Schooners, 40 feet and over.

CLASS B—Cabin Sloops and Cutters, 62 feet and
over 53 feet.

CLASS C—Cabin Sloops, 53 feet and over 45 feet.

CLASS D— " " 45 feet and over 38 feet.

CLASS E— " " 38 feet and over 32 feet.

CLASS F— " " 32 feet and over 27 feet.

CLASS G— " " all 27 feet and under.

CLASS H—All yawl rigged yachts.

CLASS 1—Open sloops, 32 feet and over 27 feet.

CLASS 2— " " 27 feet and over 23 feet.

CLASS 3— " " 23 feet and under.

CLASS 4—Cabin catrigged yachts over 23 feet.

CLASS 5— " " " 23 feet and under.

CLASS 6—Open cat rig 32 feet and over 27 feet.

CLASS 7— " " 27 feet and over 23 feet.

CLASS 8— " " 23 feet and over 20 feet.

CLASS 9— " " 20 feet and over 17 feet.

CLASS 10— " " 17 feet and under.

A Cabin Yacht shall be defined as
either an entirely flush decked vessel with
suitable cabin accomodations below deck,
or else a decked vessel with a perma-

nent fixed cabin house at least twelve inches high. All others, including those with portable summer or canvas cabins, shall be considered as open boats.

RULE II.

ALLOWANCE OF TIME.

Allowances shall be figured according to the table prepared by N. G. Herreshoff.

RULE III.

ALLOWANCE FOR RIG.

In races when boats with different rigs sail together, Yawls shall be rated for time allowance at seven-eights ($\frac{7}{8}$) of their sailing measurement.

RULE IV.

OWNERSHIP.

No two yachts owned by the some person, in whole or in part, can compete for the same prize.

FRANK W. OFELDT,

SOLE INVENTOR OF

Naphtha Systems for the Propulsion of Launches

AND MANUFACTURER OF

THE ∴ IMPROVED ∴ NAPHTHA ∴ LAUNCH,

— USING —

Steam for Power and Naphtha Gas for Fuel.

BUILDERS ALSO OF

KEROSENE AND COAL BURNING BOILERS FOR ALL PURPOSES.

WORKS,

FOOT JERSEY AVE., COMMUNIPAW, N. J.

ELLIS R. MEEKER, GENERAL AGENT.

RULE V.

ENTRIES.

Entries shall be made in the manner prescribed by the club giving the race, and the entry shall specify the name and rig of the boat, sailing length, and the owner and club to which she belongs.

RULE VI.

INSTRUCTIONS.

Each yacht entered for a race shall at the time of entry, or as soon after as possible, be supplied with written or printed instructions as to the conditions of the race, the course to be sailed, etc. Nothing shall be considered as a mark in the course unless specially named in these instructions Also, it shall be designated on which side marks and buoys shall be passed or rounded.

RULE VII.

SAILS.

Yachts in races may carry the following sails :

Schooners—Mainsail, foresail, forestay-sail, jib, flying-jib, jib-topsail, fore and main gaff-topsails, club-topsail, main topmast staysail, balloon jib and spinnaker.

Sloops and Cutters—Mainsail, forestay-sail, jib, flying-jib, jib-topsail, club-topsail, gaff-topsail, balloon jib and spinnaker.

Yawls—Same as Sloops and Cutters, with mizzen and mizzen topsail.

BALLOON SAILS.

Yachts may set light sails over working sails.

Open Sloops—Jib and mainsail only.
Catamarans—Jib and mainsail only.
Cat Boats—Mainsail only.

RULE VIII.

BALLAST, ETC.

Shifting ballast shall be allowed in open boats, but shall not be allowed in any cabin boat in any race governed by the rules of this Association, under penalty of the boat and the owner thereof, and any other boat belonging to him being debarred from further entry or participation in a race given by a club affiliated with this Association; and upon application of the sailing master or owner of a competing yacht, the judges shall order a man put aboard a yacht in the same class, said man not to count as one of the number of men allowed by the rules; said man shall not assist in any manner in working the yacht, but shall take any reasonable position the sailing master may designate; notifications to be sent by the owner or sailing master making the request to the

P. McGIEHAN, Yacht Builder,
BAYONNE, N. J.

Designer and Builder of the fastest Yachts of their day, viz: *Colleen Bawn, Rachel. Annie Mc., Mattie, Bella and Susie S., Addie Taylor, Sophia Emma, Meteor, Only Son, Lily R., Sirene, Leader,* and *Only Daughter;* also of Cabin Yachts *Kaiser Wilhelm, Meta, Cora,* of Detroit, *Ina,* of Toronto, *Cygnet,* of Buffalo, *Wild Duck,* and many others, winners of more first prizes than any yachts afloat.

committee or judges having charge, at
least four days previous to the day of the
race, and said judges or committee shall
notify the said owner or sailing master
of the yacht on which the man is to be
placed, to report on the day of the race
at the judges' boat, at least fifteen minutes previous to the starting time of the
class in which said yacht is to sail, and
only one man is to be put aboard of the
same yacht, in any one race. Any yacht
failing to comply with this rule shall be
debarred from participating in the race.

RULE IX.
CREW.

Yachts contending for prizes may carry
crew as follows :

Cabin Yachts—One man for every five
(5) feet of sailing measurement or fractional part thereof, in addition to the
sailing master.

Open Yachts—One man for every three (3) feet of sailing measurement or fractional part thereof, in addition to the sailing master.

No one shall join or leave a yacht after the start, except in case of accident or injury to any person on board.

RULE X

POSTPONEMENT OF RACE.

The Regatta Committee or officers in charge for the day, shall have power to postpone any race, should in their judgement, unfavorable weather render such course desirable.

RACES RE-SAILED.

Should any yacht duly entered for a race not start, or, having started should she withdraw or be disabled, such yacht shall be entitled to start in the event of the race being re-sailed.

NEW ENTRIES NOT TO BE RECEIVED.

No new entry shall be received under any circumstances for a postponed race.

RULE XI.

YACHTS RECEIVING PRIZES.

Before the owner of a winning yacht can receive the prize, he, or in his absence the member representimg him on the yacht, shall sign a declaration that all the rules were complied with.

RULE XII.

CLUB SIGNALS.

Each yacht shall carry her club signal at the main peak during a race.

RULE XIII.

PROPULSION.

No means of propulsion except sails, shall be employed during a race.

RULE XIV.

SOUNDING.

No other means of sounding than the hand lead and line shall be employed during a race.

RULE XV.

ANCHORING, ETC.

A yacht may anchor during a race, but must weigh her anchor again and not slip.

No yacht shall, during a race, make fast to any buoy, stage, pier, vessel or other object, or send an anchor out in a boat, except for purposes specified in Rule XVI.

RULE XVI.

RUNNING AGROUND, ETC.

A yacht running aground, or fouling a buoy, vessel or other obstruction, may use her own anchors, boats, warps, etc., to get off, but may not receive any assistance, except from the crew of the vessel fouled. Any anchor, boat or warp so used, must be taken on board again before continuing the race.

RULE XVII.

STAKE BOAT AT FINISH.

A competent person shall be placed on a stake boat at the finishing line, whose duty it shall be, in the absence of the Sailing Committee, to take the time of the yachts.

RULE XVIII.

REMOVAL OF MARKS.

Should any stake-boat, buoy or other mark be absent or moved from its proper position during a race, the race may be re-sailed or not, at the option of the Sailing Committee of the club under whose auspices the race is being sailed.

RULE XIX.

YACHTS NOT IN RACES.

All yachts not racing must keep to leeward and out of the way of racing yachts.

RULE XX.

AMENABLE TO RULES.

All yachts in a race shall be amenable to the rules from the time the preparatory signal is given.

RULE XXI.

TIME AT START AND FINISH.

The time at the start and finish shall be taken when the point marked by the foremast in schooners and the mainmast in single masted vessels and yawls crosses the line. If this point in any yacht be across the line when the signal for starting is given, she must return and re-cross the line; a yacht so returning or working into position from the wrong side of the line after the signal for starting has been given, must keep clear and give way to all competing yachts.

RULE XXII.

RIGHT OF WAY.

When one yacht is approaching another yacht, so as to involve risk of fouling, one of them shall keep clear of the other as follows ;

On Different points of sailing.

A yacht running free shall keep clear of one close hauled.

On same point of sailing with wind on opposite sides.

When both yachts are close hauled, or both free, or both have the wind aft, and having the wind on opposite sides, the yacht with the wind on the port side shall keep clear.

On same point of sailing with wind on same side.

When both yachts are free, or both have the wind aft, and have the wind on the same side, the yacht to windward shall keep clear.

Wind Aft.

A yacht with the wind aft is deemed to have the wind on the side opposite to that on which she is carrying her main boom.

A yacht with the wind aft shall keep clear of a yacht on any other point of sailing.

Overtaking.

An overtaking yacht shall, in every case, so long as an overlap exits, keep clear of the yacht which is being over-taken.

Definition of Overlap.

An overlap is established when an over-taking yacht has no longer a free choice

on which side she will pass, and continues
to exist as long as the leeward yacht by
luffing, or the weather yacht by bearing
away, is in danger of fouling.

Altering Course.

When of two yachts, one is obliged to
keep clear, the other shall not so alter
her course as to involve risk of fouling.

Luffing.

A yacht may luff as she pleases in order
to prevent another from passing her to
windward, provided she begins to luff before an overlap has been established.

Bearing Away.

A yacht shall not bear away out of her
course so as to hinder another in passing
to leeward.

Rights of New Courses.

A yacht shall not become entitled to
her rights on a new course until she has
filled away.

Converging Close Hauled.

When two yachts, both close hauled on the same tack, and converging by reason of the leeward yacht holding a better wind, and neither can claim the rights of a yacht being overtaken, then the leeward yacht shall keep clear.

Passing and Rounding Marks.

If an overlap exists between two yachts when both of them, without tacking, are about to pass a mark on a required side, then the outside yacht must give the inside yacht room to pass clear of the mark. A yacht shall not, however, be justified in attempting to establish an overlap, and thus force a passage between another yacht and the mark after the latter yacht has altered her course for the purpose of rounding.

Definition of Mark.

A mark is any vessel, boat, buoy or

other object used to indicate the course, and does not in the preceding section, involve any question of sea room.

Obstruction to Sea Room.

When a yacht is in danger of running aground, or of touching a pier, rock or other obstruction, and cannot go clear by altering her course without fouling another yacht, then the latter shall, on being hailed by the former, at once give room; and in case one yacht is forced to tack or to bear away in order to give room, the other shall also tack or bear away, as the case may be, at as near the same time as is possible without fouling.

RULE XXIII.

DISQUALIFICATION.

1. Every yacht must go fairly around the course, and must not touch any mark, but shall not be disqualified if wrongfully compelled to do so by another.

2. Any yacht causing a mark boat to in any way shift her position to avoid being fouled by such yacht shall be disqualified.

3. If a yacht, in consequence of her neglect of these rules, shall foul another yacht, or compel another yacht to foul any yacht, mark or obstruction, or to run aground, she shall be disqualified and shall pay all damages ; and any yacht which shall wrongfully cause another to luff or to bear away in order to avoid fouling, or shall, without due cause, compel another yacht to give room or to tack, under the last section of Rule XXII., or shall herself fail to tack or to bear away, as required in that section, or shall in any other way infringe or fail to comply with any of these rules, shall be disqualified.

DISQUALIFICATION WITHOUT PROTEST.

The Regatta Committee may also, without a protest, disqualify any yacht, should it come to their knowledge that she has committed a breach of these rules.

RULE XXIV.

PROTESTS.

Should a flagrant breach or infringement of these rules be proved against the owner of a yacht, he may be disqualified · by the Executive Committee of the New York Yacht Racing Association, for such time as the Executive Committee may think fit, from sailing his yacht in any race held under the rules of the Association; and should a flagrant breach of these rules be proved against any sailing master, he may be disqualified by the Executive Committee for such time as they may think fit, from sailing in any race held under these rules.

All protests and complaints must be made in writing within twenty-four hours after the close of the regatta to the Regatta Committee or officers having charge of the race.

If, through protest, the measurement of any yacht be called in question, the Regatta Committee shall direct the Measurer of the club under whose auspices the race is being sailed, to re-measure the yacht, and the result shall be reported to the Executive Committee of this Association, whose decision shall be final.

RULE XXV.

NUMBERS.

Numbers shall be black, not less than eighteen (18) inches high, on a white ground, and shall be placed on each side of the mainsail above the reef points, near mainmast.

RULE XXVI.
LIFE BUOYS.

Every cabin yacht sailing in the Regatta of this Association must carry at least two cork life buoys, placed within easy reach of the helmsman. The Regatta Committee will not award a prize to any yacht not complying with this rule.

RULE XXVII.
OTHER RULES.

The Committee in charge of a race may make rules not in conflict with the preceding.

RULE XXVIII.
AMENDMENTS.

These rules and regulations may be amended by a two-thirds vote at any meeting of the Association; provided, however, that the notice of the meeting shall have contained the proposed amendment in full.

*TABLE OF ALLOWANCES.

Length.	Allowance.	Length.	Allowance.	Length.	Allowance.	Length.	Allowance.
12	5 29.0	15	4 43.9	18	4 9.5	21	3 41.9
1	5 27.4	1	4 42.8	1	4 8 6	1	3 41.2
2	5 26.0	2	4 41.7	2	4 7.8	2	3 40.5
3	5 24 6	3	4 40.7	3	4 7 0	3	3 39.9
4	5 23.2	4	4 39.6	4	4 6.1	4	3 39.2
5	5 21.8	5	4 38.6	5	4 5.3	5	3 38.5
6	5 20.5	6	4 37.6	6	4 4.5	6	3 37.9
7	5 19.1	7	4 36.5	7	4 3.6	7	3 37.2
8	5 17.7	8	4 35.5	8	4 2.8	8	3 36.5
9	5 16.4	9	4 34.5	9	4 2.0	9	3 35.9
10	5 15.0	10	4 33.5	10	4 1.2	10	3 35.2
11	5 13.7	11	4 32.5	11	4 0.4	11	3 34.5
13	5 12.4	16	4 31.5	19	3 59.6	22	3 33.9
1	5 11.1	1	4 30.5	1	3 58 8	1	3 33.2
2	5 9.8	2	4 29.5	2	3 58.0	2	3 32.6
3	5 8.6	3	4 28.5	3	3 57.3	3	3 32.0
4	5 7.3	4	4 27.5	4	3 56.5	4	3 31.3
5	5 6.0	5	4 26.5	5	3 55.7	5	3 30.7
6	5 4.8	6	4 25.6	6	3 55.0	6	3 30.1
7	5 3.5	7	4 24.6	7	3 54.2	7	3 29.4
8	5 2.3	8	4 23.7	8	3 53.4	8	3 28.8
9	5 1.1	9	4 22 8	9	3 52.7	9	3 28.2
10	4 59.9	10	4 21.8	10	3 51.9	10	3 27.5
11	4 58.7	11	4 20.9	11	3 51.2	11	3 26.9
14	4 57.5	17	4 20.0	20	3 50.5	23	3 26 3
1	4 56.3	1	4 19.1	1	3 49.7	1	3 25.7
2	4 55.1	2	4 18.2	2	3 49.0	2	3 25.1
3	4 53.9	3	4 17.3	3	3 48.3	3	3 24.5
4	4 52.7	4	4 16.4	4	3 47.5	4	3 23.9
5	4 51.6	5	4 15.5	5	3 46.8	5	3 23.3
6	4 50.5	6	4 14.6	6	3 46.1	6	3 22.7
7	4 49.4	7	4 13.7	7	3 45.4	7	3 22.1
8	4 48.3	8	4 12 8	8	3 44.7	8	3 21.5
9	4 47.2	9	4 12.0	9	3 44.0	9	3 20.9
10	4 46.1	10	4 11.1	10	3 43.3	10	3 20.3
11	4 45.0	11	4 10.3	11	3 42.6	11	3 19.7

TABLE OF ALLOWANCES.

Length.	Allowance.	Length.	Allowance.	Length.	Allowance.	Length.	Allowance.
24	3 19.2	27	3 0.0	30	2 43.4	33	2 28.9
1	3 18.6	1	2 59.5	1	2 42.9	1	2 28.5
2	3 18.0	2	2 59.0	2	2 42.5	2	2 28.1
3	3 17.5	3	2 58.5	3	2 42.1	3	2 27.7
4	3 16.9	4	2 58.0	4	2 41.7	4	2 27.3
5	3 16.3	5	2 57.5	5	2 41.3	5	2 27.0
6	3 15.8	6	2 57.0	6	2 40.9	6	2 26.7
7	3 15 2	7	2 56.5	7	2 40.4	7	2 26.3
8	3 14.6	8	2 56.0	8	2 40.0	8	2 25.9
9	3 14.1	9	2 55.6	9	2 39 6	9	2 25.5
10	3 13.5	10	2 55.1	10	2 39.2	10	2 25.1
11	3 12.9	11	2 54.6	11	2 38.8	11	2 24.8
25	3 12.4	28	2 54 2	31	2 38.4	34	2 24.5
1	3 11.8	1	2 53.7	1	2 37.9	1	2 24.1
2	3 11.3	2	2 53.2	2	2 37.5	2	2 23.7
3	3 10.8	3	2 52.8	3	2 37.1	3	2 23.3
4	3 10.2	4	2 52.3	4	2 36.7	4	2 22.9
5	3 9.7	5	2 51.8	5	2 36.3	5	2 22.6
6	3 9.2	6	2 51.4	6	2 35.9	6	2 22.3
7	3 8.6	7	2 50.9	7	2 35.5	7	2 21.9
8	3 8.1	8	2 50.4	8	2 35.1	8	2 21.5
9	3 7.6	9	2 50.0	9	2 34.7	9	2 21.1
10	3 7.0	10	2 49.5	10	2 34.3	10	2 20.8
11	3 6.5	11	2 49.0	11	2 33.9	11	2 20.5
26	3 6.0	29	2 48.6	32	2 33.5	35	2 20.2
1	3 5.5	1	2 48.1	1	2 33.1	1	2 19.8
2	3 5.0	2	2 47.7	2	2 32.7	2	2 19.4
3	3 4.5	3	2 47.3	3	2 32.3	3	2 19.0
4	3 4.0	4	2 46.8	4	2 31.9	4	2 18.7
5	3 3.5	5	2 46.4	5	2 31.5	5	2 18.4
6	3 3 0	6	2 46.0	6	2 31.2	6	2 18.1
7	3 2.5	7	2 45.5	7	2 30.8	7	2 17.7
8	3 2.0	8	2 45.1	8	2 30.4	8	2 17.3
9	3 1.5	9	2 44.7	9	2 30.0	9	2 17.0
10	3 1.0	10	2 44.2	10	2 29.6	10	2 16.7
11	3 0.5	11	2 43.8	11	2 29.2	11	2 16.4

TABLE OF ALLOWANCES.

Length.	Allowance.	Length.	Allowance.	Length.	Allowance	Length.	Allowance.
36	2 16.1	39	2 4.6	42	1 54.2	45	1 44.9
1	2 15.7	1	2 4.3	1	1 53.9	1	1 44.6
2	2 15.3	2	2 4.0	2	1 53.6	2	1 44.3
3	2 15.0	3	2 .3.7	3	1 53.3	3	1 44.0
4	2 14.7	4	2 3.4	4	1 53.0	4	1 43.8
5	2 14.4	5	2 3.1	5	1 52.8	5	1 43.6
6	2 14.1	6	2 2.8	6	1 52.6	6	1 43.4
7	2 13.7	7	2 2.5	7	1 52.3	7	1 43.1
8	2 13.3	8	2 2.2	8	1 52.0	8	1 42.8
9	2 13.0	9	2 1.9	9	1 51.7	9	1 42.5
10	2 12 7	10	2 1.6	10	1 51.4	10	1 42.3
11	2 12.4	11	2 1.3	11	1 51.2	11	1 42.1
37	2 12.1	40	2 1.0	43	1 51.0	46	1 41.9
1	2 11.7	1	2 0.7	1	1 50.7	1	1 41.5
2	2 11.4	2	2 0.4	2	1 50.4	2	1 41.3
3	2 11.1	3	2 0.1	3	1 50.1	3	1 41.0
4	2 10.8	4	1 59.8	4	1 49.8	4	1 40.8
5	2 10.5	5	1 59.5	5	1 49.6	5	1 40 6
6	2 10.2	6	1 59.3	6	1 49 4	6	1 40.4
7	2 9.5	7	1 59.0	7	1 49.1	7	1 40.1
8	2 9.5	8	1 58.7	8	1 48.8	8	1 39.8
9	2 9.2	9	1 58.4	9	1 48 5	9	1 39.6
10	2 8.9	10	1 58.1	10	1 48.3	10	1 39.4
11	2 8.6	11	1 57.8	11	1 48.1	11	1 39.2
38	2 8.3	41	1 57.6	44	1 47 9	47	1 39.0
1	2 7.9	1	1 57.3	1	1 47.6	1	1 38.7
2	2 7.6	2	1 57.0	2	1 47.3	2	1 38.4
3	2 7.3	3	1 56.7	3	1 47.0	3	1 38.2
4	2 7.0	4	1 56 4	4	1 46.8	4	1 38.0
5	2 6.7	5	1 56.1	5	1 46.6	5	1 37.8
6	2 6.4	6	1 55.9	6	1 46 4	6	1 37.6
7	2 6.1	7	1 55.6	7	1 46.1	7	1 37.3
8	2 5 8	8	1 55 3	8	1 45.8	8	1 37.0
9	2 5.5	9	1 55.0	9	1 45.5	9	1 36.8
10	2 5 2	10	1 54.7	10	1 45 3	10	1 36.6
11	2 4.9	11	1 54.4	11	1 45.1	11	1 36 4

TABLE OF ALLOWANCES.

Length.	Allowance.	Length.	Allowance.	Length.	Allowance.
48	1 36.2	56	1 16.4	88	0 23.7
1	1 35.9	6	1 15.3	89	0 22.5
2	1 35.6	57	1 14.2	90	0 21.3
3	1 35.4	6	1 13.1	91	0 20.1
4	1 35.2	58	1 12.0	92	0 18.9
5	1 35.0	6	1 10.9	93	0 17.8
6	1 34.8	59	1 9 8	94	0 16.7
7	1 34.5	.6	1 8.8	95	0 15.6
8	1 34.3	60	1 7.8	96	0 14.5
9	1 34.1	61	1 5.8	97	0 13.4
10	1 33.9	62	1 3.8	98	0 12 3
11	1 33.7	63	1 1.9	99	0 11.2
49	1 33.5	64	1 0.0	100	0 10.2
1	1 33.2	65	0 58.1	101	0 9.2
2	1 33.0	66	0 56.3	102	0 8.2
3	1 32.8	67	0 54.5	103	0 7.2
4	1 32.6	68	0 52.8	104	0 6.2
5	1 32.4	69	0 51.1	105	0 5.2
6	1 32.2	70	0 49.4	106	0 4.2
7	1 31.9	71	0 47.8	107	0 3.3
8	1 31.7	72	0 46.2	108	0 2.4
9	1 31.5	73	0 44.6	109	0 1.5
10	1 31 3	74	0 43.0	110	0 0.6
11	1 31.1	75	0 41.5	6	0 0.0
50	1 30.9	76	0 40.0		
6	1 29.6	77	0 38 5		
51	1 28.3	78	0 37.0		
6	1 27.0	79	0 35.6		
52	1 25.8	80	0 34.2		
6	1 24.6	81	0 32.8		
53	1 23 4	82	0 31.4		
6	1 22.6	83	0 30.1		
54	1 21.0	84	0 28.8		
6	1 19.8	85	0 27.5		
55	1 18.6	86	0 26.2		
6	1 17.5	87	0 24.9		

To reduce a yacht's time to the time for the standard length find in the table the number of minutes and seconds corresponding to the sailing length of the yacht, and multiply it by the distance in miles sailed; subtract this product from the actual time.

* This Table is calculated by Mr. Herreshoff for statute Miles.

Officers New York Yacht Racing Association.

1889.

President,
ALANSON J. PRIME,
Commodore Yonkers Corinthian Yacht Club.

Vice President,
FREDERICK W. PANGBORN,
Jersey City Yacht Club.

Secretary,
GEORGE PARKHILL,
Columbia Yacht Club.

Treasurer,
ROBERT K. McMURRAY.
Staten Island Athletic Club.

Executive Committee,

W. W. WASHBURN......Sing Sing Yacht Club.
CHAS. W. VOLTZ ......Williamsburgh Yacht Club.
JAMES F. LALOR.. .....Harlem Yacht Club.
GEO. E. GARTLAND ...New Jersey Yacht Club.
CHAS. E. CAMERON....Newark Yacht Club.

Regatta Committee,

GEO. PARKHILL,	R. PUHLMAN,
CHAS. E. CAMERON,	B. S. GIBSON,

J. K. TUCKER.

Officers New York Yacht Racing Association.

1890.

President,
ALANSON J. PRIME,

Vice President,
CHAS. E CAMERON.

Secretary,
GEORGE PARKHILL.

Treasurer,
ROBERT K. McMURRAY.

Executive Committee,
E. B. SHERWOOD.......Sing Sing Yacht Club
JAMES F. LALOR.......Harlem Yacht Club.
GEO. E. GARTLAND ....New Jersey Yacht Club.
H. B. PEARSON ....Jersey City Yacht Club.
R. V. FREEMAN.........Hudson River Yacht Club.

Regatta Committee,

GEORGE PARKHILL,	R. PUHLMAN,
THOS. E. BOOTH,	J. A. STYLES,
E. M. GROVER.	

Officers New York Yacht Racing Association.
1891.

President,
ALANSON J. PRIME,

Vice President,
GEORGE E. GARTLAND.

Secretary,
GEORGE PARKHILL,

Treasurer,
ROBERT K. McMURRAY,

Executive Committee,

E. B. SHERWOOD.......Sing Sing Yacht Club.

CHAS. E. SIMMS, JR ...Columbia Yacht Club.

H. B. PEARSON ....Jersey City Yacht Club.

CHAS. E. CAMERON....Newark Yacht Club.

WM. A. SMITH.........Pavonia Yacht Club.

Regatta Committee,

GEO. E. GARTLAND,   CHAS. E. SIMMS, JR.,
WILLLIAM CAGGER.

—FIRST ANNUAL REGATTA—

OF THE

New York Yacht Racing Association.

SUMMARY.

Sailed Monday, September 2nd, 1889.

CLASS D—CABIN SLOOPS.

COURSE I—Forty-five and Over Thirty-eight Feet.

NAME.	OWNER.	Length.		Start.	Finish.	Elapsed.	Allowance.	Corrected.
		FT.	IN.	H. M. S	H. M. S.	H. M. S.	M. S.	H. M. S.
*Gertrude	Com. H. B. Pearson	38	6	12 26 53	6 42 34	6 15 41	52 40	5 23 01
Avalon	L. Mittlesdorf	38	11	12 24 11	did not finish		52 2	
Phantom	Com. D. W. Kohn	38	2	12 24 29	"	"	53 10	
Dudley	W. J. Knight et al	41	6	12 24 53	"	"	48 17	

CLASS E—CABIN SLOOPS.

COURSE II—Thirty-eight and over Thirty-two Feet.

NAME.	OWNER.	Length.		Start.	Finish.	Elapsed.	Allowance.	Corrected.
		FT.	IN.	H. M. S	H. M. S.	H. M. S.	M. S.	H. M. S.
*Mergus	N. Com. W H Rowe	34	7	12 27 46	5 32 36	5 04 50	47 18	4 17 32
Carrie Van Vorhees	W. Pinckeney	35	0	12 21 51	5 28 39	5 06 48	46 44	4 20 04
Emma and Alice	D. McGlynn	32	6	12 30 00	6 08 45	5 38 45	50 24	4 48 21
Lottie	J E. Drew	32	9	12 22 22	6 12 06	5 49 44	50 24	4 59 20
Caprice	E. M Grover	35	9	12 28 39	6 17 36	5 48 57	45 40	5 03 17
Tam O'Shanter	A. McInnes	35	11	12 21 53	6 12 00	5 49 07	45 28	5 03 39
Agnes S	C. Schwanke	34	8	12 29 13	6 22 39	5 53 26	47 10	5 06 16
Katie Louiss	Com. Roth	32	4	12 21 20	6 27 24	6 06 04	50 38	5 15 26
Emily B	L. Abbett, Jr	33	1	12 24 53	6 31 46	6 06 53	49 30	5 17 23
Coquette	M. J. Charde	34	0	12 28 37	6 43 55	6 13 18	48 10	5 27 08
Wacondah	H. Doscher	32	2½	12 25 05			49 18	

CLASS F—CABIN SLOOPS.

COURSE II—*Thirty-two and over Twenty-seven Feet.*

NAME	OWNER	Length		Start	Finish	Elaps'd	Allowance	Corrected
		FT.	IN.	H. M. S.	H. M. S.	H. M. S.	M. S.	H. M. S.
*Forsyth	A. F. Roe	29	6	12 22 07	5 33 20	5 11 13	55 20	4 15 53
Emmy C	C. E. Cameron	31	6	12 26 55	6 07 08	5 40 13	51 58	4 48 15
Jonah	J. F. Hitchcock	28	2½	12 30 00	6 45 25	6 15 25	57 40	5 17 45
Progress	J. Scheussele	31	10	12 30 00	6 51 09	6 21 09	51 26	5 29 43
Julian	J. Nightingale	28	7	12 21 21	did not finish.		56 58	
Restless	F. Weslow	29	8	12 23 06	"	"	55 02	
Peerless	Com. J. F. Lalor	30	5	12 23 40	"	"	53 46	
Wabasso	G. L. Winn	28	6	12 26 27	"	"	57 08	
Annie R	T. J. Rache	27	5	12 27 22	"	"	59 10	
Gracie T	L. M. Little	31	4	12 30 00	"	"	52 14	

CLASS G—CABIN SLOOPS.

COURSE III—*Twenty-seven Feet and Under.*

NAME	OWNER	Length		Start	Finish	Elaps'd	Allowance	Corrected
		FT.	IN.	H. M. S.	H. M. S.	H. M. S.	M. S.	H. M. S.
*Lurline	H. C. Rosemund	25	6	12 26 01	5 07 10	4 41 09	47 18	3 53 51
Bertha	A. Skinner	26	3½	12 22 53	5 02 48	4 39 55	46 03	3 53 52
Christine	S. A. Chester	25	6	12 25 35	5 21 59	4 56 24	47 18	4 09 06
Empire	E. Sulzer	24	1	12 26 05	5 34 44	5 08 39	49 39	4 19 00
Nellie C	T. Coburn	22	6	12 25 37	5 48 47	5 23 10	52 31	4 30 39
Hattie	L. M. Poland	25	9	12 24 17	5 44 45	5 20 28	46 54	4 33 34
Arrow	A. F. Wobcke	25	6	12 24 51	did not finish.		47 18	
Flirt	H. C. Schwarz	23	10½	12 28 45	"		50 00	

CLASS 1—OPEN SLOOPS.

COURSE III—*Thirty-two and over Twenty-seven Feet.*

NAME.	OWNER.	Length		Start.			Finish.			Elapsed.			Allowance.		Corrected.		
		FT.	IN.	H.	M.	S.	H.	M.	S.	H.	M.	S.	M.	S.	H.	M.	S.
*Amateur........	Com. F. Burritt..	30	00	12	36	05	4	21	16	3	45	11	40	51	3	04	20
Eagle Wing........	J. B. Scott........	27	10	12	37	15	4	55	49	4	18	34	43	46	3	34	48

CLASS 2—OPEN SLOOPS.

COURSE III—*Twenty-seven and over Twenty-three Feet.*

NAME.	OWNER.	Length		Start.			Finish.			Elapsed.			Allowance.		Corrected.		
*James T. Corlett..	C. Rothmal........	26	4½	12	34	23	4	12	49	3	38	26	45	55	2	52	31
Gesine............	V. C, W. Lutters..	23	10½	12	37	12	4	42	06	4	04	54	50	00	3	14	54
Our Own..........	C. S. Braisted....	23	10	12	32	29	4	49	42	4	17	13	50	04	3	27	09
Thorn	W. E. Kinzey......	24	5	12	35	10	5	04	39	4	29	29	49	04	3	40	25
Eunice...........	T. Meyers.........	23	1	12	32	14	did not		finish.				51	25			

CLASS 3—OPEN SLOOPS.

COURSE IV—*Twenty-three and over Twenty Feet.*

NAME.	OWNER.	Length		Start.			Finish.			Elapsed.			Allowance.		Corrected.		
*Rival............	Com. F. Burritt..	21	00	12	38	05	3	50	11	3	12	06	44	23	2	27	43
Just Woke Up......	J. D. Phillips......	21	9	12	38	12	4	11	34	3	33	22	43	11	2	50	11
Sophia............	T. McDonnell......	21	9	12	32	58	4	16	35	3	43	37	43	11	3	00	26
Gypsie............	J. C. Ebmeyer.....	20	6	12	34	15	4	39	36	4	05	21	45	13	3	20	08
Leader	O. M. Rau	22	4	12	40	00	did not		finish.				42	16			

CLASS 4—OPEN SLOOPS.
COURSE IV – *Twenty Feet and under.*

NAME.	OWNER.	Length FT. IN.	Start H. M. S.	Finish H. M. S.	Elaps'd H. M. S.	Allowance M. S.	H. M. S.
*Lone Star......	A. Bauer......	18 3	12 40 00	4 28 04	3 48 04	49 24	2 58 40
Mascotte......	G. S. Brown......	17 10	12 40 00	did not finish.		50 13	

CLASS 5—CABIN CAT BOATS.
COURSE III.

NAME.	OWNER.	Length FT. IN.	Start H. M. S.	Finish H. M. S.	Elaps'd H. M. S.	Allowance M. S.	H. M. S.
*Bessie......	G. Van Horne......	31 00	12 37 14	4 47 25	4 10 11	39 36	3 30 35
Ella F.......	J. Dixon......	27 2	12 34 40	4 51 55	4 17 15	44 45	3 32 30
Ripple......	F. Muller......	22 6	12 37 00	5 40 31	5 03 31	52 31	4 11 00
Venture......	J. T. Martin......	20 4	12 39 59	did not finish		56 52	

CLASS 6—OPEN CAT BOATS
Over Twenty-seven and under *Thirty-two Feet.*
COURSE—Same as for Class G. Distance – 15 nautical miles.

NAME.	OWNER.	Length FT. IN.	Start H. M. S.	Finish H. M. S.	Elaps'd H. M. S.	Allowance M. S.	H. M. S.
*Nora L.......	J. H. Levings......	28 00	12 39 33	4 58 15	4 18 41	43 33	3 35 08
Nina......	Com Prime......	30 5¼	12 33 57	4 50 10	4 16 13	40 16	3 35 57
Elvira......	W. H. Prodgers, Jr.	27 6	12 36 51	4 55 05	4 20 14	44 15	3 35 59
Square......	R. Pringle......	27 4	12 34 05	4 59 41	4 25 36	44 30	3 41 06

CLASS 7—OPEN CAT BOATS.
COURSE III – *Twenty-seven and over Twenty-three Feet.*

NAME.	OWNER.	Length FT. IN.	Start H. M. S.	Finish H. M. S.	Elaps'd H. M. S.	Allowance M. S.	H. M. S.
*Alida......	C. F. Vreeland......	23 9	12 34 12	4 49 55	4 15 43	50 13	3 25 30
Aller......	P. F. Sainstag......	25 9¼	12 33 21	4 56 42	4 23 22	46 49	3 36 33
S. × Free......	E. Clark......	26 3	12 35 30	5 00 15	4 24 45	46 07	3 38 38
Irene......	R. Murray......	24 1	12 31 20	5 05 07	4 33 47	49 39	3 44 08
Maoy F.......	J. A. Styles......	24 9¼	12 30 20	did not finish		48 27	

CLASS 8 – OPEN CAT BOATS.
Course IV—*Twenty-three and over Twenty Feet.*

NAME.	OWNER.	Len'th.		Start.			Finish.			Elaps'd.			Allowance.		Corrected.		
		FT.	IN.	H.	M.	S.	H.	M.	S.	H.	M.	S.	M.	S.	H.	M.	S.
*Pauline B	C. S. Raymond	22	6½	12	31	36	3	57	20	3	25	44	41	56	2	43	48
Lizzie V	W. P. Vreeland	21	4	12	36	33	4	06	01	3	29	28	43	40	2	45	38
F. Oliver	W. Arndt	21	5	12	40	00	4	10	57	3	30	57	43	42	2	47	15
H. H. Holmes	A. I. Kreymeyer	22	4	12	34	49	4	14	51	3	40	02	42	16	2	57	46
Irex	R. M. Haddock	22	7½	12	32	24	4	13	21	3	40	57	41	49	2	59	08
Emma D	C. Dreyer	20	3½	12	32	19	4	17	03	3	44	44	45	35	2	59	09
Three Brothers	R. Stemer	22	3	12	33	29	4	18	39	3	45	10	42	24	3	02	46
Mary S	J. W. Shaughnessy	22	1	12	34	15	4	29	25	3	55	10	42	38	3	12	32
Shamrock	E McEvoy	22	8	12	37	00	3	34	05	3	57	05	41	46	3	15	19

CLASS 9—OPEN CAT BOATS.
Course IV—*Twenty Feet and under.*

NAME.	OWNER.	Len'th.		Start.			Finish.			Elaps'd.			Allowance.		Corrected.		
		FT.	IN.	H.	M.	S.	H.	M.	S.	H.	M.	S.	M.	S.	H.	M.	S.
*Bon Ton	E. M. Post	18	00	12	34	54	4	07	35	3	32	41	49	54	2	42	47
Go Softly	E. S. Wheeler, jr.	19	11½	12	35	39	4	13	07	3	37	28	46	10	2	51	18
So So	A. L. Vreeland	19	11½	12	34	23	4	16	53	3	42	30	46	10	2	56	20
Ida K	C. W. Voltz	19	11	12	33	32	4	16	24	3	42	52	46	14	2	56	38
Trioton	W. B. Adams	18	9	12	35	00	4	37	09	4	02	09	48	24	3	14	35
Henry Fisher	M. Nickolaus	19	4	12	40	00	4	44	02	4	04	02	47	18	3	16	44
Hoo Doo	J. Woods	19	11½	12	36	59	4	46	02	4	09	03	46	10	3	22	53
Mirlam	B. Barnett	18	1	12	38	00							49	43	4	16	18
Gaunlet	R. M. Jones	19	10	12	34	00	5	44	01	5	06	01	46	23			
Dash	H. H. Silling	15	6	12	37	18							55	31			
Addie				12	40	00											

All boats marked thus * were winners in their respective classes.

SECOND ANNUAL REGATTA

OF THE

New York Yacht Racing Association.

Sailed Monday, September 1st, 1890.

SUMMARY.

CLASS C—CABIN SLOOPS.

Fifty-three Feet and over Forty-five Feet.

NAME.	OWNER.	Sailing Length.	Allowance.	Start.	Finish.	Elapsed Time.	Corrected Time.
		FT. IN.	M. S.	H. M. S.	H. M. S.	H. M. S.	H. M. S.
*Dolphin	Com. H. F. Allen..	48 11½	37 26 04	12 15 10	7 22 13	7 07 03	6 29 36 6

CLASS D—CABIN SLOOPS.

Forty-five Feet and over Thirty-eight Feet.

NAME.	OWNER.	Sailing Length.	Allowance.	Start.	Finish.	Elapsed Time.	Corrected Time.
*Avalon.............	L. Mittelsdorf......	39 03	49 28 08	12 22 00	7 14 14	6 52 14	6 02 45 2
Gertrude............	H. B. Pearson......	38 06	50 33 06	12 21 55	7 16 15	6 54 20	6 03 46 4
Phantom	Com. D. W. Kohn...	38 02½	50 57 06	12 17 41	7 15 20	6 57 39	6 06 41 4

CLASS E—CABIN SLOOPS.

Thirty-eight Feet and over Thirty-two Feet.

NAME.	OWNER.	Sailing Length	Allowance.	Start.	Finish.	Elapsed Time.	Corrected Time.
		FT. IN.	M. S.	H. M. S.	H. M. S	H. M. S.	H. M. S.
*Mergus	Com. W. H. Rowe	34 07	56 45 06	12 20 58	7 15 30	6 54 32	5 57 46 4
Nimrod	Com. L. Abbett, Jr.	35 03	55 36 00	12 21 45	7 15 30	6 53 45	5 58 09 0
Orestes	Thos. J. Rache	36 06	53 38 04	12 22 00	7 17 00	6 55 00	6 01 21 6
Volusia	J. M. Williams	35 00	56 04 08	12 15 00	7 14 45	6 59 45	6 03 40 2

CLASS F—CABIN SLOOPS.

Thirty-two Feet and over Twenty-seven Feet.

NAME.	OWNER.	Sailing Length	Allowance.	Start.	Finish.	Elapsed Time.	Corrected Time.
		FT. IN.	M. S.	H. M. S.	H. M. S	H. M. S.	H. M. S.
*Forsyth	Alex. Roe	29 09	1 05 52 8	12 19 22	7 16 24	6 57 02	5 51 09 2
Pavonia	Jno. Mellor	27 07	1 10 36 0	12 13 21	7 18 10	7 04 49	5 54 13 0
Maud M	W. W. McManus	27 03	1 11 24 0	12 13 13	7 19 50	7 06 37	5 55 13 0
Peerless	Com. T. F. Lalor	30 06	1 04 21 6	12 15 50	7 16 10	7 00 20	5 55 58 4
Brunehilde	Chas. T. Wills	28 08	1 08 09 6	12 17 40	7 23 30	7 05 50	5 57 40 4
Mascot	David Loper	31 05½	1 02 24 0	12 19 01	7 32 03	7 13 02	6 10 38 0
Emmy C	Chas. E. Cameron	31 04	1 02 40 8	12 14 20	did	not	finish.
Annie R	Thos. J. Rache	27 05½	1 10 50 4	12 22 00	"	"	"

CLASS G—CABIN SLOOPS.

Twenty-seven Feet and Under.

NAME.	OWNER.	Sailing Length. FT. IN.	Allowance. H. M. S	Start. H. M. S	Finish. H. M. S	Elapsed Time. H. M. S.	Corrected Time. H. M. S.
†Millie	C. H. Benson	24 04	1 02 21 1	12 15 15	6 09 00	5 53 45	4 51 23 9
*Christine No.1	W. A. Smith	25 06	59 54 8	12 19 13	6 11 00	5 51 47	4 51 52 2
Theresa	A. W. Warner	25 01½	1 00 38 5	12 14 38	6 07 30	5 52 52	4 52 13 5
Souter Johnnie	A. McInness	26 10	57 19 0	12 17 15	6 (9 20	5 52 05	4 54 46 0
Bertha	A. L. Skinner	26 00¾	57 00 6	12 16 15	6 12 30	5 36 15	4 59 14 4
Christine No. 2	C. F. Stevens	22 05	1 06 43 3	12 22 00	7 20 10	6 58 10	5 51 26 7
Maud	E. A. Morley	24 06	1 02 00 2	12 22 00	7 17 03	6 55 03	5 53 2 8
Vixen	Jno. Dickson	26 06½	57 53 2	12 22 00	7 16 50	6 54 50	5 56 56 8
Aunt Jennie	R. H. McFarland	23 06	1 04 11 3	12 22 00	did	not	finish.

CLASS 1 OPEN SLOOPS.—*Twenty-seven Feet and Over Twenty-three Feet.*

NAME.	OWNER.	Sailing Length. FT. IN.	Allowance. H. M. S	Start. H. M. S	Finish. H. M. S	Elapsed Time. H. M. S.	Corrected Time. H. M. S.
Helen	L. M. Kayser	29 00	53 23 4	did	not	finish.	......
*Eagle Wing	Com. J. B. Scott	27 10	55 26 9	12 24 46	6 21 45	5 56 59	5 01 32 1

CLASS 2—OPEN SLOOPS.—*Twenty-seven Feet and over Twenty-three Feet.*

NAME.	OWNER.	Sailing Length. FT. IN.	Allowance. H. M. S	Start. H. M. S	Finish. H. M. S	Elapsed Time. H. M. S.	Corrected Time. H. M. S.
‡Our Own	J. J. Vree'and	24 00	1 03 04 8	12 30 00	5 23 39	4 53 39	3 50 34 2
*Jno. A. Cameron	J. J. McCarthy	26 02½	58 31 2	12 24 30	5 16 10	4 51 40	3 53 08 8
Carrie B	G. S. Brown	24 08	1 01 37 4	12 29 30	5 52 57	5 23 27	4 21 49 6
Beulah	H. A. Young	26 06	57 57 0	12 29 05	6 14 20	5 45 15	4 47 18 0
Lizzie F	M. Flynn	26 06	57 57 0	12 32 00	7 15 50	6 43 50	5 45 53 0
Jas. T. Corlett	C. Rothmal	26 04½	58 12 2	did	not	finish.	

CLASS 3—OPEN SLOOPS.
Twenty-Three Feet and Under.

NAME.	OWNER.	Sailing Length FT. IN.	Allowance. H. M. S.	Start. H. M. S.	Finish. H. M. S.	Elapsed Time. H. M. S.	Corrected Time. H. M. S.
*Just Woke Up	J. Phillips	22 06	49 01 4	12 32 00	4 16 40	3 44 40	2 55 38 6
H. C. Miner	David McGlynn	16 05	1 02 11 0	12 32 00	4 32 05	4 00 05	2 57 54 0
Leader	Otto Rau	22 04	49 18 2	12 27 22	4 22 40	3 55 18	3 05 59 8
Schemer	Wm. Faas	18 04	57 25 4	12 23 40	5 27 41	5 04 01	4 06 35 6
Louis W	Wm. A. White	22 00	49 54 6	12 27 14	5 28 11	5 00 57	4 11 02 4

CLASS 4—CABIN CAT BOATS.
Over Twenty-three Feet.

NAME.	OWNER.	Sailing Length FT. IN.	Allowance. H. M. S.	Start. H. M. S.	Finish. H. M. S.	Elapsed Time. H. M. S.	Corrected Time. H. M. S.
†Henry Gray	Orlieb & McArdle	26 00	58 54 0	12 25 40	6 16 11	5 50 31	4 51 37 0
*Edna	E. L. Phillips	25 00¾	1 00 48 0	12 24 40	7 16 35	6 51 55	5 51 07 0
Lona	Ed. Davis	26 00	58 54 0	12 28 14	7 20 50	6 52 36	5 53 42 0
Storme Childe	Theo. Meyer	27 06	56 03 3	12 24 20	7 15 31	6 51 11	5 55 07 7
Nina	Com. A. J. Prime	30 06	50 57 1	12 27 12	7 18 30	6 51 18	6 00 20 9

CLASS 5—CABIN CAT BOATS.
Twenty-three Feet and Under.

NAME.	OWNER.	Sailing Length FT. IN.	Allowance. H. M. S.	Start. H. M. S.	Finish. H. M. S.	Elapsed Time. H. M. S.	Corrected Time. H. M. S.
*Ripple	Fred. Muller	22 06	49 01 4	12 32 10	5 25 30	4 53 20	4 04 18 6
May Bee	J. K. Tucker	20 05	52 55 2	12 25 32	6 10 03	5 44 31	4 51 35 8

CLASS 6 – OPEN CAT BOATS.

Thirty-two Feet and over Twenty-seven Feet.

NAME.	OWNER.	Sailing Length	Allowance.	Start.	Finish.	Elapsed Time.	Corrected Time.
		FT. IN.	M. S.	M. H. S.	H. M. S	H. M. S.	H. M. S.
*Norah L	J. H. Levings	28 00	55 09 8	12 36 42	5 12 50	4 36 08	3 40 58 2
Square	Pringle&McCaffrey	27 04	56 22 00	12 37 40	did	not	finish.

CLASS 7—OPEN CAT BOATS.

Twenty-seven Feet and over Twenty-three Feet.

NAME.	OWNER.	Sailing Length	Allowance.	Start.	Finish.	Elapsed Time.	Corrected Time.
*Nadeya	F. L. Degraw	25 00	1 00 55 6	12 33 40	5 15 50	4 42 10	3 41 14 4
May F	J. A. Styles	24 9¼	1 01 26 0	12 32 50	5 55 35	5 20 45	4 19 19 0
Vivid	Jas. Dorsey	24 7	1 01 48 8	12 33 20	6 15 50	5 42 30	4 40 41 2
Irene	Robt. Murray	24 01	1 02 53 4	12 34 40	7 07 40	6 33 00	5 30 06 8
Gesine	Wm. Lutters	23 10½	1 03 2C 7	12 38 00	7 19 45	6 41 45	5 38 24 3
Marie	Frank Barth	24 03½	1 02 23 0	12 36 42	did	not	finish.

CLASS 8—OPEN CAT BOATS.—*Twenty-three Feet and over Twenty Feet.*

NAME.	OWNER.	Sailing Length FT. IN.	Allowance. M. S.	Start. H. M. S.	Finish. H. M. S.	Elapsed Time. H. M. S.	Corrected Time. H. M. S.
*Undine	Clinton R. James	21 10	50 12 8	12 34 35	4 29 35	3 55 00	3 04 47 2
Oneita	F. S. Jeaks	22 04½	49 14 0	12 34 37	4 36 19	4 01 42	3 12 28 0
Eureka	Wm. Durham	21 10	50 12 8	12 34 12	4 37 25	4 03 13	3 13 00 2
Lizzie B.	Com. G. A. Bonker	21 11¾	49 58 8	12 34 00	4 37 52	4 03 52	3 13 53 2
Three Brothers	Connoly & Steurer	22 02	49 36 4	12 34 38	4 41 18	4 06 40	3 17 03 6
Pauline B	J. R. Smith	22 7⅞	48 47 4	12 33 33	4 52 35	4 19 02	3 30 14 6
Orient	A. R. Osborn	22 1¾	49 38 5	12 33 29	4 53 40	4 20 11	3 30 32 5
Frank Oliver	Wm. Arndt	22 04½	51 03 2	12 37 32	5 00 30	4 22 58	3 31 54 8
Columbia	L. T. Washburn, Jr.	21 04½	48 51 6	12 34 13	5 01 15	4 27 02	3 38 10 4
Irma	F. H. Whitney	22 0	49 54 6	12 34 39	did not	not	finish.

CLASS 9—OPEN CAT BOATS.—*Twenty Feet and over Seventeen Feet.*

NAME.	OWNER.	Sailing Length FT. IN.	Allowance. M. S.	Start. H. M. S.	Finish. H. M. S.	Elapsed Time. H. M. S.	Corrected Time. H. M. S.
*Bon Ton	E. M. Post	18 0	58 13 0	12 33 10	4 15 15	3 42 05	2 43 52 0
Rival	Chas. J. Hart	19 11	53 56 8	12 40 11	4 29 50	3 49 39	2 55 42 2
Dolphin	H. C. Schwarz	19 6	54 50 0	12 40 10	4 32 19	3 52 09	2 57 19 0
Mist	Jos. Sandford	17 10	58 35 4	12 36 19	4 35 30	3 59 11	3 00 35 6
Anita	W. P. Vreeland	19 06	54 50 0	12 35 09	4 31 30	3 56 21	3 01 31 0
Chas. T. Wills	M. Nichols	19 04	55 11 0	12 37 45	4 39 59	4 02 14	3 07 03 0
Gauntlet	E. M. Jones	19 11	53 56 8	12 34 01	4 37 53	4 03 52	3 09 55 2
Merllen	Chas. Muller	20 0	53 47 0	12 35 50	did not	not	fir.1sh.

CLASS 10—OPEN CAT BOATS.—*Seventeen Feet and Under.*

NAME.	OWNER.	Sailing Length FT. IN.	Allowance. M. S.	Start. H. M. S.	Finish. H. M. S.	Elapsed Time. H. M. S.	Corrected Time. H. M. S.
Galoawater	J. Spavin	16 01½	49 30	12 27 35	4 27 40	3 50 05	3 00 34

All boats marked thus * were winners in their respective classes. † Improperly classified. ‡ Disqualified.

THIRD ANNUAL REGATTA

OF THE

New York Yacht Racing Association.

Sailed Monday, September 7th, 1891.

SUMMARY.

CLASS D —Course I.—Sloops 45 feet and over 38 feet.

NAME.	Sailing Len'th.	Time Allowance (Standard)	OWNER.	Start.	Finish.	Elaps'd Time.	Correct-ed time.
	FT. IN.	H. M. S.		H. M. S.	H. M. S.	H. M. S.	H. M. S.
*Notus	41 6	46 21-6	Com. Wm. H. Rowe	12 30 00	4 44 02	4 14 02	3 27 40-4
Avalon	39 7	49 0	L. Mittelsdorf	12 30 00	5 59 45	5 29 45	4 40 45
Gertrude	38 6	50 33-6	H. B. Pearson	12 30 00	4 50 29	4 20 29	3 29 55-4

CLASS E—Course I—Sloops 38 feet and over 32 feet.

NAME.	Sailing Len'th.	Time Allowance (Standard)	OWNER.	Start.	Finish.	Elaps'd Time.	Correct-ed time.
Orestes	36 6	58 38-4	Thos. J. Rache	12 22 58	5 42 36	5 19 38	4 25 59-6
*Carrie V. Voorhees	34 8	56 36	John H. Thorne	12 21 40	5 26 36	5 04 56	4 08 20
Nautilus	34 0	57 48	Prtugle & Haskin	12 23 06	5 38 09	5 15 03	4 17 15
Agnes S	34 0	57 48	Chas. Schwanke	12 25 31	6 02 30	5 36 59	4 39 11
Lottie	33 6	58 40-8	John E Drew	12 23 37	6 01 10	5 37 33	4 38 52-2
Emma and Alice	32 8	1 00 00-0	David McGlyn	12 30 00	did not finish.		
Katie Louise	32 4½	1 00 43-2	Henry Roth	12 21 20	5 52 25	5 31 05	4 30 21-8

CLASS F —COURSE I—Sloops 32 feet and over 27 feet.

Yacht	ft	in			Owner	Start	Finish	Elapsed	Corrected	
Progress	31	10¾	1 01	40-8	James Schuessele	12 23 38	did not finish.			
Emmy C	31	7½	1 02	07-2	Chas. E. Cameron	12 20 46	5 37 28	5 16 42	4 14	34-8
Mascott	31	5¾	1 02	24-0	D. Loper	12 21 30	6 12 02	5 50 32	4 48	08
Seybolt	31	1	1 03	05-6	W. P. Willis	12 20 54	5 29 58	4 59 04	3 55	58-4
Peerless	30	6	1 04	21-6	Jas. F. Lalor	12 30 00	did not finish.			
Prince Karl	30	1	1 05	09-6	S. J. Meeker	12 29 08	6 01 30	5 32 22	4 27	12-4
*Bessie (yawl)...†	30	0	1 13	51	G. Van Horn	12 22 40	5 07 49	4 45 09	3 31	18
Forsyth	29	10	1 05	40-8	Alex. F. Roe	12 23 34	5 19 17	4 55 43	3 50	02-2
Smuggler*	29	10½	1 07	43-2	Fred. W. Wright et al.	12 22 25	disabled.			
Pavonia	28	06	1 08	33-6	Jas. Johnston et al.	12 30 00	did not finish.			

CLASS G —COURSE II—Sloops 27 feet and under.

Yacht	ft	in			Owner	Start	Finish	Elapsed	Corrected	
Soutter Johnnie	26	08	57	38	A. McInness	12 30 00	did not finish.			
Bertha	26	0¾	58	42-6	A. L. Skinner	12 30 00	5 48 30	5 18 30	4 19	47-4
Christine	25	06	59	54-8	Smith & Chester	12 28 52	5 34 29	5 05 37	4 05	42-2
Deer	24	08	1 01	37-4	Oscar Reed	12 24 52	did not finish.			
*Christina	22	07	1 06	18-6	Charles Stevens	12 30 00	did not finish.			

CLASS 2 —COURSE II—Open Sloops 27 feet and over 23 feet.

Yacht	ft	in		Owner	Start	Finish	Elapsed	Corrected
J. T. Cameron	26	4	58 16	John McCarthy	12 36 36	5 35 10	4 58 34	4 00 18
Viola	25	3	1 00 25	Wm. L. Bachmeyer	12 37 17	did not finish, capsized.		
*Carrie B	24	8	1 01 37-4	Gilbert S. Brown	12 33 20	5 20 15	4 46 55,3	45 17-6

CLASS 3 —COURSE III—Open Sloops 23 feet and under.

Yacht	ft	in		Owner	Start	Finish	Elapsed	Corrected
*Leader	22	4	49 18-2	Otto M. Rau	12 33 34	4 32 10	3 58 36,3	09 17-8
Oceola	19	0	55 54-4	Alex. Cochrane	12 40 00	did not finish.		

CLASS 4—COURSE II—Cabin Cat Boats over 23 feet.

Boat				Owner				
Ella F	27	6¾	56	01-1	Quick & Dickson	12 37 45	5 07 48	4 30 03	3 34 01-9
Storm Child	27	6	56	03	Theo. Meyers	12 32 22	did not finish.		
*Henry Gray	26	02	58	35-0	Ortlieb & McArdle	12 32 50	5 03 59	4 31 09	3 32 03-4
Charm 2	26	0	58	54	Peter V. Giffin	12 37 09	did not finish.		
Water Lily	26	0	58	54	Zimmerman & Hoffman	12 32 23	5 19 05	4 46 02	3 47 48
Vespa	25	11	59	03-5	James F. Fielder	12 38 45	did not finish.		
Edna	25	00	1 00	55-6	Edward L. Phillips	12 39 16	5 22 25	4 43 09	3 42 13-4
Vivid	24	10½	1 01	08-9	James Dorsey	12 32 15	6 10 32	5 38 17	4 37 08-1
Guile	24	6	1 02	00-2	L. F. McNett	12 30 46	did not finish.		
Falcon	24	5	1 02	09-7	Whitney & Romaine	12 37 11	5 29 50	4 52 39	3 50 29-3

CLASS 5—COURSE III—Cabin Cat Boats 23 feet and under.

Boat				Owner				
Annie J	23	0	48	08-2	George W. James	12 40 00	5 07 58	4 27 58	3 39 49-8
*Mary Anna	22	10	48	25	T. H. Throop	12 40 00	4 45 14	4 05 14	3 16 49
Ripple	22	9½	48	29-2	Fred Muller	12 31 40	dismasted		
Brunette	22	1½	49	39-2	Chris. Walden	12 40 00	5 50 40	5 10 40	4 31 00-8
Restless	21	10	50	12-8	Mersereau & Cochrane	12 40 00	4 55 10	4 15 10	3 24 57-2
Mohican	19	8	54	27-6	F. H. Davis	12 33 32	did not finish.		
Ada	18	13	58	13	Frank M. Randall	12 40 00	5 10 15	4 30 15	3 32 02

CLASS 6—COURSE II—Open Cat Boats 32 feet and over 27 feet.

Boat				Owner				
*Norah L	28	0	55	09-8	James H. Levings	12 44 49	6 03 08	5 18 19	4 23 09-2
Square	27	4	56	22	Richard Pringle	12 46 24	did not finish.		

CLASS 7—COURSE II—Open Cat Boats 27 feet and over 23 feet.

Boat				Owner				
*Only Daughter	25	0	1 00	55-6	Theo. H. Rogers	12 44 50	4 47 00	4 02 10	3 01 14-4
May F	24	9¾	1 01	22-2	J A. Styles	12 41	7 dismasted		
Henry Dauer	24	5½	1 02	00	Dougherty & McCabe	12 41	3 5 07 17	4 26 14	3 24 14
Irene	24	1	1 02	53-4	Robert Murray	12 44	00 did not finish.		
Bona Fide	24	0	1 03	04-8	J. J. Murphy	12 49	5 5 34 01	4 44 10	3 41 05-2

CLASS 8—COURSE III—Open Cat Boats 23 feet and over 20 feet.

Boat	ft	in			Owner	Start	Finish	Elapsed	Corrected
Shamrock	22	8	48	43-2	Eugene Parker	12 40 49	did not finish.		
*Pauline B	22	7½	48	47-4	Charles S. Raymond	12 43 42	4 03 41	3 19 59	2 31 11-6
Mary S	22	0	49	54-6	T. J. & J W. Shaughnessy	12 41 47	4 39 03	3 57 16	3 07 21-4
Lizzie B	21	11½	49	58-8	Com. Geo. A. Bouker	12 44 48	4 09 15	3 24 27	2 34 28-2
Eureka	21	10	50	12-8	R. E. Relyea & Wm. Durham	12 43 30	4 14 00	3 30 36	2 40 23-2
Homing	21	8	50	31	Ed. F. Drayton	12 41 02	4 17 32	3 36 30	2 45 59

CLASS 9—COURSE III—Open Cat Boats 20 feet and over 17 feet.

Boat	ft	in			Owner	Start	Finish	Elapsed	Corrected
Torment	20	00	53	47	Wm. Hongwont	12 43 18	4 29 0	3 45 42	2 51 55
Golden Rod	20	00	53	47	Edward McEvoy	12 40 45	did not finish.		
Rival	19	11	53	56-8	F. H. Hegler	12 40 00	did not finish.		
Katrina	19	10	54	06-6	Falkenstein & Lober	12 45 45	4 59 20	4 13 35	3 19 28-4
Evelene B	19	10	54	06-6	Com. Albert Beale	12 41 45	4 46 52	4 05 07	3 11 00-4
*Ges So	18	05	57	14-2	Joseph Elsworth	12 46 53	4 27 25	3 40 32	2 43 17-8
My Partner	18	01	58	00-4	C. J. Lutton	12 41 07	did not finish.		
Bon Ton	18	00	58	13	E. M. Post	12 42 18	did not finish.		

CLASS 10—COURSE IV—Open Cat Boats 17 feet and under.

Boat	ft	in			Owner	Start	Finish	Elapsed	Corrected
*Gracie	16	6	48	41-6	J. H. Stevenine	12 42 04	4 01 35	3 19 31	2 30 49-4
Essex	16	6	48	41-6	Joseph Sandford	12 48 35	did not finish.		
Ileen	16	3½	48	08	H. J. Ritchie	12 42 18	5 01 25	4 19 07	3 29 59
Gala Water	16	2	49	24-5	John Spavin	12 42 18	did not finish.		
Jessie A	15	8	50	30-5	Chas. Wimmer	12 45 35	did not finish.		
Harry C	15	0	52	02-9	William Porter	12 46 57	4 19 45	3 32 48	2 40 45-1

All boats marked thus * were winners in their respective classes.

SPAR VARNISH.

85 Marlboro, CHELSEA, MASS.,

June 1st, 1891.

MESSRS. BERRY BROTHERS, Detroit, Mich.

GENTLEMEN : The thirty-foot yacht "Neversink," in which I sailed from New York via Boston to the Paris Exposition in 1889, had her spars and deck finished with your Spar Varnish. I am now using it for my new boat, the "Sea Serpent," fifteen feet long, in which I will start from Boston, June 17th, for a race across the Atlantic with Capt Wm. A. Andrews, of the "Mermaid."

The conditions and exposure are exceptionally severe; and the fact of my again selecting "BERRY BROTHERS' Spar Varnish" shows that I consider it the best made, and all that is claimed for it.

Josiah W. Lawton

The letter shown above should be of especial interest to Yacht men, as it bears convincing testimony to the merits of our Spar Varnish.

Insist upon getting *Berry Brothers' Spar Varnish.* You will be pleased with it.

BERRY BROTHERS, Varnish Manufacturers.

NEW YORK, 252 Pearl St.,   BOSTON, 42 Pearl St.,   FACTORY—Detroit.

STEAM VESSEL AND YACHT AGENCY.

M. HUBBE,
NAVAL ARCHITECT
—AND—
MARINE ENGINEER,
22 STATE STREET,

Telephone, 3542 Cortlandt.   NEW YORK

All classes of Steam Vessels, Steam Yachts, etc. modeled and designed for steel, iron, wood or composite, their costruction superintended or contracted for, complete ready for service.

LIGHT DRAFT VESSELS A SPECIALTY.

FOR SALE AND CHARTER.—Large selections of Steam and Sailing Yachts, Launches, Towboats, Freight and Passenger Steamers, and Vessel property in general.

Owners desiring to sell, will find this Agency a reliable and quick medium by sending fullest particulars. No charges made unless a sale is effected.

www.ingramcontent.com/pod-product-compliance
Lightning Source LLC
Chambersburg PA
CBHW021413090426
42742CB00009B/1130